A SHORT GUIDE TO THE BIBLE

EXPLORING THE MOST IMPORTANT BOOK YOU'LL EVER READ

KATY MORGAN
ILLUSTRATED BY PATRICK LAURENT

A Short Guide to the Bible
© The Good Book Company, 2025, Reprinted 2025.
thegoodbook.co.uk | thegoodbook.com | thegoodbook.com.au | thegoodbook.co.nz
Illustrated by Patrick Laurent
Katy Morgan has asserted her right to be identified as author of this work.
Unless indicated, Scripture references are taken from the Holy Bible,
New International Version. Copyright © 2011 Biblica, Inc.™ Used by permission.
ISBN: 9781802542998 | JOB-008370 | Printed in Turkey

WELCOME to the BIBLE

Since you're reading this, I'm guessing you are at least a little bit interested in knowing about God. And you think that the Bible is a good place to find out about him. (You're right.)

Maybe you also want to know about how to be a good person and live a happy life. And you think the Bible might have something to say about that too. (Right again!)

BUT WHERE DO YOU START?

The Bible isn't like any other book you've ever read. It's huge, and the writing is tiny. There are not very many fun facts or laugh-out-loud jokes or exciting cliffhangers. And it all happened a very long time ago.

How are you supposed to read a book like that?

This guide is designed to help!

TRUE OR FALSE?

1. The Bible is the best-selling book in the world.
2. The oldest surviving copy of a bit of the Bible dates to about 600 BC.
3. The Bible is the most banned book in the world.
4. The Bible was written in three different languages, across three continents.
5. The Bible is actually a library of 66 books.
6. Parts of the Bible have been translated into 3,658 different languages (so far).
7. The Bible was the very first book to be printed using a printing press (instead of written out by hand).
8. Cats are the animal mentioned most often in the Bible.

*They're all true except the last one. Lions and leopards are mentioned, but ordinary cats never appear!

In the following pages, you'll find everything you need to get going with reading the Bible (except an actual copy of the Bible).

You'll find out that the Bible is really one big story. It tells you about God, it tells you about the world, and it even tells you about you!

You'll learn about how the Bible divides up into different parts, and what those parts are.

There are also maps of Bible places, info about Bible characters, and answers to your most confusing questions!

But most importantly, this guide aims to help you enjoy the Bible and get the most out of it. Because it isn't like any other book you've ever read. It's much, much, *much* more special.

IT'S GOD, WHO MADE THE UNIVERSE, SPEAKING TO YOU!

FINDING YOUR WAY AROUND

Step ❶ Get a Bible

Make sure you have an actual Bible, not a story Bible. You can tell the difference by looking to see if it has little numbers all over the text. If it does, it's a Bible!

Step ❷ Flip to the Contents Page

You'll probably see that it's divided into two sections: the Old Testament and the New Testament. Basically, the Old Testament is the story of God's people before Jesus came along, and the New Testament is the story of God's people after Jesus came along. (More on Jesus later!)

Step ❸ Pick a Book and Flip To It

The names you see in the contents page are the books—Genesis, Exodus, and so on. It doesn't matter which one you choose!

Have a look at the numbers. The big ones are chapter numbers. Within each chapter, there are also tiny verse numbers. The whole Bible is divided into bite-sized verses so that you can easily find the bit you want.

Step ❹ Find a Verse

Look at chapter 1 of the book you're in. Can you find verse 4 of this chapter? What does it say?

> You're unlikely to find people writing "verse 4 of chapter 1". Instead they shorten it to 1 v 4 or 1:4 or 1.4.
>
> Exodus 9 v 10 = Exodus, chapter 9, verse 10
> Mark 11 v 13-15 = Mark, chapter 11, verses 13 to 15
> Nehemiah 2 = Nehemiah, chapter 2 (the whole chapter!)

NOW SEE IF YOU CAN FOLLOW THE SAME STEPS AND FIND THE FOLLOWING VERSES:

Psalm 139 v 13

Genesis 1 v 1**

John 3 v 16*

Matthew 11 v 1-4

*Be careful to find John, not 1 John or 2 John or 3 John! Confusing, I know...

**Watch out—the first verse of each chapter usually doesn't have a verse number. It just follows straight on from the chapter number!

Well done! Now you know how to read the Bible.

A BOOK I LOVE

I find that the best way to study the Bible is to read 3-4 verses a day, ask yourself questions about what you have read, and then pray about it.

Kiara (age 13)

I love that God speaks to me in so many different ways through the Bible, even if I'm reading the same thing over and over again.

Evie (age 10)

Every time you read it, the Bible teaches you a bit more about God's power and love. I love that it tells you how to pray and how to forgive.

Rio (age 11)

THE WHOLE BIBLE AT A GLANCE

You might have heard about specific Bible stories and characters. But did you know that the Bible tells the story of God's plan for the whole world and its people?

God Creates the World
It's perfect, but the first humans ruin it by disobeying God.

God Chooses a People
The nation of Israel will represent him to the world.

People Keep Messing Up
Israel is supposed to be a place of justice and peace. Sadly, most of the time, the humans get in the way...

God Rescues His People
The Israelites have become slaves in Egypt, but he gets them out and gives them a land of their own.

God Punishes His People
Powerful empires invade and take God's people away into exile.

God Promises Something Better

The people return to their own land, but things aren't as good as before. They're longing for God to sort out all their problems! He says he will.

THIS IS WHERE THE OLD TESTAMENT ENDS. THE LAST OLD TESTAMENT BOOK WAS WRITTEN IN ABOUT 400 BC. THAT'S 400 YEARS BEFORE THE NEW TESTAMENT BEGINS!

Jesus Arrives

He is God himself, come to earth as a human, to sort everything out. Jesus tells people how to live and demonstrates God's power.

Jesus Dies and Rises Again

Right from the start, this was God's plan to rescue not just the Israelites but the whole world.

Christianity Spreads

Jesus' friends spread the news that anyone can be forgiven and become part of God's people if they trust in Jesus.

YOU ARE HERE!

God Remakes the World

One day, everyone who trusts in Jesus will get to be part of a perfect new creation.

HOW DID WE GET THE BIBLE?

The Bible has 66 books—and many different authors. Christians believe that God's Holy Spirit spoke to the Bible writers and made sure they wrote what was true.

1 Stories and Scribes

The earliest Bible books were written down thousands of years ago. They were written on scrolls which wore out quickly, so new copies would be made to replace them. This copying process carried on all the way into medieval times.

2 Hebrew Scriptures

The Old Testament was completed a few hundred years before Jesus. It was written in Hebrew (apart from some short bits in Aramaic).

For a long time, the oldest surviving copies of the Old Testament were ones that dated from the 9th century AD—a long time after it was first written. But in 1947, archaeologists found hundreds of ancient scrolls in some jars in a cave. They come from the 1st century BC and include some complete Old Testament books! These ancient copies were almost exactly the same as the more recent copies. Apart from a few small errors, the words hadn't been changed at all.

3 Adding Greek

Within 100 years after Jesus' death, everything in the New Testament had been written. This time it was all written in Greek—which was a language spoken by lots of people from lots of different places. The Bible's message was spreading across the world!

4 Language Barrier

The Bible was copied by lots of scribes, monks and nuns throughout many centuries—mostly in Latin. In the 1300s, a man named John Wycliffe translated the whole Bible into English for the first time. His translation was banned! But 200 years later, Henry VIII commanded that every church in England should have a whole Bible in English. Today, there are hundreds of different English translations available.

BIBLE WRITERS

Some Bible books have named authors. For example, here's how the writer Paul identifies himself (and his readers) in his letter to the Ephesians:

"Paul, an apostle of Christ Jesus by the will of God,
  To God's holy people in Ephesus, the faithful in Christ Jesus."

Others are more of a mystery! For example, there is a lot of debate about who the author of Ecclesiastes was. He just identifies himself as "the Teacher"!

UNDERSTANDING TRANSLATIONS

Languages don't match each other exactly. This makes translation difficult! Every translator makes a slightly different choice about the best way to get across the original meaning in the new language. For example, here's something Jesus said in Luke 23 v 43. The original Greek looks like this (with the meaning of each word underneath):

ἀμήν	σοι	λέγω	σήμερον	μετ' ἐμοῦ	ἔσῃ	ἐν	τῷ παραδείσῳ
truly	to you	I say	today	with me	you will be	in	paradise

New International Version: Truly I tell you, today you will be with me in paradise.
King James Bible: Verily I say unto thee, Today shalt thou be with me in paradise.
Good News Translation: I promise you that today you will be in Paradise with me.

All these are accurate translations, but they sound quite different to us!

THE **OLD** TESTAMENT

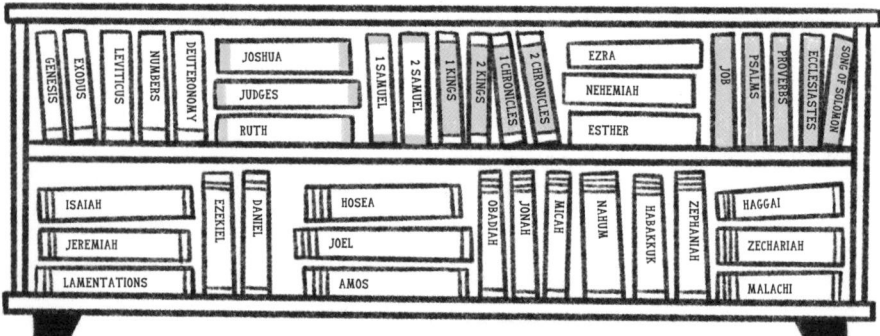

HISTORY

- ### From the Beginning... — Genesis, Exodus, Leviticus, Numbers, Deuteronomy

  The first five books of the Bible tell the story of God's people up until they left slavery in Egypt, including the laws God gave them. They are sometimes called the Pentateuch (which means Five Books) or Torah (which means Law).

  TRY GENESIS 12

- ### Judges and Kings — Joshua, Judges, Ruth, 1 Samuel, 2 Samuel

  These five books cover the period when the Israelites were settling in their new land and becoming a nation, including their first few kings. They're full of interesting characters and exciting stories.

  TRY 1 SAMUEL 17

- ### More Kings (mostly bad ones) — 1 Kings, 2 Kings, 1 Chronicles, 2 Chronicles

  These books cover the whole history of God's people up until they went into exile. They overlap with some of the stories told in previous books, but add lots more too!

  TRY 1 KINGS 17

- ### Israel in Exile — Ezra, Nehemiah, Esther

  Each of these books tells a single story from when the Israelites were in exile and then when they returned to the promised land. (The book of Daniel could fit in this category too.)

  TRY NEHEMIAH 2

POETRY and WISDOM

Job, Psalms, Proverbs, Ecclesiastes, Song of Solomon

These books are all quite different to each other! Instead of telling stories, they contain big thoughts about who God is, what the world is like and how to live well.

> TRY PSALM 23 AND PROVERBS 4

PROPHETS

Prophets are people who speak a message from God for a particular time and place. They're tied to moments in history, but provide warnings and encouragements for us today too.

• The Big Ones   Isaiah, Jeremiah, Lamentations, Ezekiel, Daniel

These are known as "the major prophets"—not because they're the most important but because they're the longest! They were written around the time when Israel was threatened by invasion and exile.

> TRY ISAIAH 40

• The Little Ones   Hosea, Joel, Amos, Obadiah, Jonah, Micah, Nahum, Habakkuk, Zephaniah, Haggai, Zechariah, Malachi

More messages from God, written to particular people at particular times. The odd one out here is Jonah, which reads more like a history book.

> TRY JOEL 2

DIVE IN

Try looking up the chapters listed in each section above. Then you can say you've read something from every part of the Old Testament! You might not understand every word, but that's okay. As you read, try praying to God and asking him to show you something about himself.

THE NEW TESTAMENT

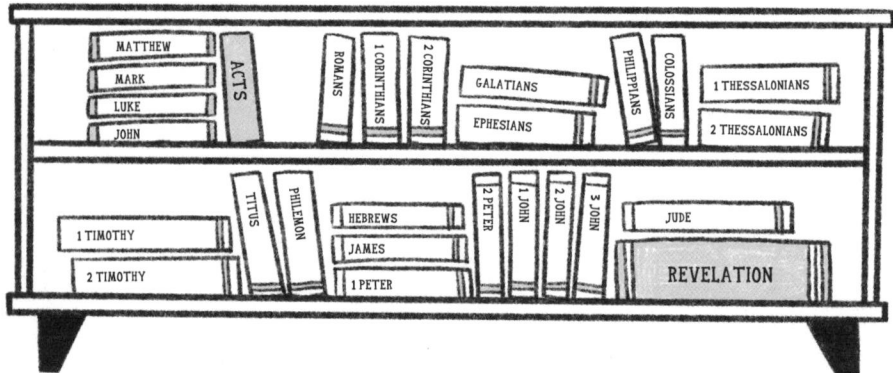

HISTORY

- ### Good News — Matthew, Mark, Luke, John

    These books are known as Gospels. Each one tells the story of Jesus' life. "Gospel" means "good news"!

    > TRY MARK 1 AND JOHN 9

- ### The Message Spreads — Acts

    Written by the same person as Luke's Gospel, this book starts soon after Jesus' resurrection. It describes how the good news about Jesus spread and the number of his followers grew and grew.

    > TRY ACTS 12

LETTERS

- ## With Love from Paul
  Romans, 1 and 2 Corinthians, Galatians, Ephesians, Philippians, Colossians, 1 and 2 Thessalonians, 1 and 2 Timothy, Titus, Philemon

  Paul was one of the leaders of the early church, and he did a lot of letter-writing! Each of these books is written to a specific community of Christians (e.g. the ones in Rome or the ones in Corinth), or to an individual friend (e.g. Timothy). These letters contain lots of teaching about Jesus and how to follow him.

  > TRY PHILIPPIANS 1

- ## Other Letters
  Hebrews, James, 1 and 2 Peter, 1, 2 and 3 John, Jude

  While Paul's letters are named after the people who received them, most of these letters are named after the people who sent them! The author of Hebrews is unknown, but most of the others are signed off by their authors. Like Paul's letters, these books contain teaching about living life as Christians.

  > TRY 2 JOHN

THE END
Revelation

The final book of the Bible is also a letter, but it's pretty different to the rest. It uses lots of symbolic language, which can be difficult to make sense of! But overall, it shows us that God is in control of the whole of history. And it tells us about the perfect future that all Christians look forward to.

> TRY REVELATION 21

NEW HEAVENS NEW EARTH

DIVE IN

If you want to try reading the Bible but you're not sure where to start, Mark is a good place. Try reading a short chunk at a time. For each chunk, ask yourself: what am I learning about Jesus here?

You can read the Old Testament this way too. Jesus is the most important person in the Bible, and even Old Testament passages can tell us something about him. Sometimes somebody does something that's like what Jesus would later do. Sometimes the story just shows us how much the world needed Jesus to come!

USEFUL BIBLE VERSES

Got questions? Or maybe you're just feeling like you need some words to help you through your day. Try looking up the following verses and find out what God says about whatever you're thinking about.

GETTING TO KNOW GOD

Jesus' mission: Isaiah 53; Luke 4 v 18-19; Revelation 5 v 9-10

God's forgiveness: 2 Chronicles 7 v 14

God's grace: Ephesians 2 v 8-9

God's love for sinners: Titus 3 v 3-7

God's judgment: Psalm 34 v 21-22

God's patience: 2 Peter 3 v 8-9

God's protection: Psalm 91

God's will for us: Romans 12 v 1-2

God's wisdom: Romans 11 v 33-36

The Holy Spirit: John 14 v 16-17

LIVING LIFE WITH GOD

HELP FOR WHEN I'M FEELING...

Becoming like Jesus: 2 Corinthians 3 v 17-18

Boasting: Jeremiah 9 v 23-24

Difficult people: Luke 6 v 27-36

Doing the right thing: 2 Corinthians 8 v 21

Enemies: Romans 12 v 19-21

Eternal life: John 17 v 3; Revelation 14 v 13

Evangelism: Romans 10 v 14-15

Faith: Hebrews 11 v 1

Living for Jesus: Titus 2 v 11-14

Love: 1 Corinthians 13; Romans 8 v 38-39

Money & possessions: Matthew 6 v 19-21

Persecution: Matthew 10 v 16-20

Perseverance: Hebrews 12 v 1-3

Prayer: Luke 11 v 1-13; 1 John 5 v 14-15

Serving others: Matthew 20 v 25-28

Temptation: 1 Corinthians 10 v 13

Truth: John 8 v 31-32

Wisdom: James 3 v 17

Afraid: Psalm 23; Psalm 27 v 1

Angry: Ephesians 4 v 26-27

Doubtful: Mark 9 v 23-24; John 20 v 24-31

Guilty: 1 John 1 v 9

Jealous: Psalm 37 v 1-4; 1 Timothy 6 v 6-10

Lonely: John 14 v 15-21

Not good enough: Romans 4 v 4-5

Not strong enough: 2 Corinthians 4 v 16; 2 Corinthians 12 v 9

Sad: Revelation 21 v 3-4

Worried: Matthew 6 v 31-34; 1 Peter 5 v 7

ADD YOUR OWN USEFUL VERSES

A Very Helpful Habit

Many people find it helpful to read the Bible regularly as a way of growing in their faith. But how do you do that—and keep doing it? Here are some top tips…

Pray About It!

God wants to speak to us through the Bible—so you can always start by asking for his help if you're feeling unsure (and even if you're not!). Jesus said, "The Holy Spirit, whom the Father will send in my name, will teach you all things" (John 14 v 26). So, all you need to say is, "Father God, please send me the Holy Spirit to teach me about what I read in the Bible." (You can find out more about the Holy Spirit towards the end of this booklet.) Then, after you've finished reading, ask for God's help again.

A Chunk at a Time

There's no need to read lots of the Bible at once. Sometimes you'll find there's plenty to chew on in just a single verse! Don't be afraid to go as slowly as you need. And, if you find that you're confused by the bit of the Bible you've started reading, don't worry—just move on. There's plenty of Bible to read, and a whole lifetime to figure it out.

Time and Place

If you really want to build a habit of Bible-reading, it's probably a good idea to set aside a specific time and place when you'll always open the Bible. Maybe it's every Sunday morning while you eat breakfast in the kitchen, or maybe it's every night, tucked up in bed.

The time and place I choose is:

Ask These Questions

Try asking these questions to help you get the most out of what you've read.

What's happening?
Literally, what's going on? Or (if it's not a story) what is being said? Can you sum it up in a few sentences?

What does it tell me about God/Jesus?
Sometimes it will literally tell you something: "God is ____." Other times you'll need to look more carefully—asking questions like: What is God doing here? What is he like? How do people react to him?

What does it mean for me?
Sometimes this is really obvious: it says, "Do this!" But even when it's not obvious, there's always something we can take away into our own lives. God uses the Bible to shape how we live—so ask yourself, "What will I do now that I've read this?"

Get Creative

You don't have to just sit there reading. You can be creative! Make a doodle of a Bible verse you like. Draw pictures to illustrate a story. Invent a song to help you remember a verse you've read. Listen to an audio Bible while you're on the way to somewhere. Or anything else you'll enjoy!

Read It Together

If you're unsure about reading the Bible on your own, that's okay! Try reading it with a friend and figuring it out together. Or ask a youth leader at a local church. You can also buy Bible notes to help guide you through your reading—look in the back of this booklet to discover some!

MEET JESUS

FACT FILE

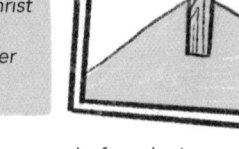

NAME: Jesus

Jesus is sometimes called "Jesus Christ". The word Christ isn't a surname—it's a title, like Mr or Lord. It means "God's chosen one" or "God's promised king". Another Bible word that means the same thing is "Messiah".

BORN: Bethlehem, in around AD 1 (or maybe a few years before that)

DIED: Jerusalem, in around AD 33 (about 2,000 years ago)

APPEARANCE: You'll often see Jesus depicted with a dark brown beard and wavy hair, but the truth is that nobody knows for sure what Jesus looked like—just like with most people who lived before photography was invented.

JOB: Carpenter, then a wandering teacher. And now, the ruler of the world!

Christians believe that Jesus is the Son of God. He always existed, but then he came to earth as a human baby, lived a normal life, and died on a cross. And that wasn't the end: he came back to life again! Jesus is now in heaven with God the Father, and one day he will return to the earth and make everything new.

Have you ever seen a date with BC or AD written next to it? They're both to do with Jesus. BC means "Before Christ". AD stands for Anno Domini, which is Latin for "The Year of the Lord"—that is, a year when Jesus rules the world! That's ALL years, ever since he rose from the dead.

FAQs:

Did Jesus really exist?

Yes—historians agree on this, including ones who don't believe that Jesus was the Son of God!

Was Jesus a human?

Yes—the Bible makes it clear that he was completely, 100% human, just like you and me. Except, he was also completely 100% God! He wasn't half-god, half-human like some characters in Greek mythology. He was God, become human. (More on this later.)

Why did Jesus die and rise again?

The Bible tells us that humans' relationship with God is broken. God is wonderful and perfect, and we aren't! Jesus came in order to fix that relationship. When he died, he was taking the punishment for all of the things we do wrong. When he rose again, it was a sign that his plan had succeeded! Now, those who trust in Jesus can have a perfect friendship with God.

DIVE IN: Who is Jesus?

The Bible says that Jesus is God, but we also read about lots of people trying to make up their mind about whether that's true. Have a look at the following passages where people meet Jesus. (There are seven, so you could read one per day for a week if you like.)

What do each of them think about him? What do YOU think about him?

- The man who couldn't walk: Mark 2 v 1-12
- The scared sailors: Mark 4 v 35-41
- The home-town haters: Mark 6 v 1-6
- The mountaintop marvel: Mark 9 v 2-10
- The precious perfume: Mark 14 v 3-9
- The confused governor: Mark 15 v 1-15
- The amazed soldier: Mark 15 v 25-39

A BIBLE WHO'S WHO

There are at least 2,000 named characters in the Bible! Including 6 Marys, 13 Josephs and 31 Zechariahs. But only one Melchizedek (which we should probably be grateful for). Here are just a few of the most important.

Adam and Eve (Genesis 2-4)

The first humans! God created these two right at the beginning of the world. He gave them everything they needed, but they chose to distrust and disobey him. Every human born after them would do the same.

Abraham and Sarah (Genesis 12-25)

Originally called Abram and Sarai. God promised them that they would have as many descendants as there are stars in the sky! All of the Israelites were descended from them. And the Bible tells us that if we have faith in Jesus, we are Abraham's "children" too.

Moses (Exodus)

Moses was minding his own business as a shepherd in the desert when God spoke to him out of a burning bush! God sent Moses to lead his people out of slavery in Egypt.

Deborah (Judges 4-5)

Deborah was a prophet (someone God speaks to), and people came to her to sort out their disagreements and problems. She saved Israel from oppression by instructing army commander Barak to lead a rebellion against the king of Canaan!

David (1 Samuel 16 - 2 Samuel 24 and 1 Chronicles 11 - 29)

David was just a boy looking after sheep when God chose him to be the future king of Israel! He won lots of battles and made Israel into a strong nation. He was also a great musician and wrote lots of the Psalms.

Elijah (1 Kings 17 – 2 Kings 2)

God sometimes chose people to be his messengers (or prophets). Elijah was one of those. Many of God's people were worshipping false gods, led by their evil king and queen. Elijah told people they should worship God alone!

Esther (Esther)

God's people had been scattered throughout the huge Persian Empire. Esther was a young woman who ended up becoming queen! She courageously stood up to the king and saved God's people from being destroyed.

Mary and Joseph (Matthew 1 – 2 and Luke 1 – 2)

Jesus' earthly parents. They were engaged, but not yet married, when an angel appeared to Mary and told her that she would have a baby that came from God. Mary and Joseph were ordinary people, not rich or famous—Joseph was a carpenter.

The twelve disciples (Matthew, Mark, Luke, John and Acts)

Jesus had many followers while he was on earth, but he chose 12 men in particular to be his disciples or apprentices. They went with him everywhere. Peter is the most famous!

Paul (Acts 8 – 28 and many letters)

Also known as Saul. He hated the followers of Jesus, but one day he experienced Jesus for himself, and his life was changed. He spent the rest of his life talking about Jesus and trying to persuade others to follow him. Paul wrote many of the letters in the New Testament.

Know all those? Here are a few more characters whose stories you might enjoy.

Hagar was met by God in the wilderness. (Genesis 16 v 7-13)
Nebuchadnezzar went mad and ate grass. (Daniel 4 v 29-37)
Nicodemus came to Jesus in the dead of night. (John 3 v 1-21)
Eutychus was raised back to life after falling out of a window. (Acts 20 v 7-12)

THE WHOLE BIBLE AT A GLANCE (AGAIN)

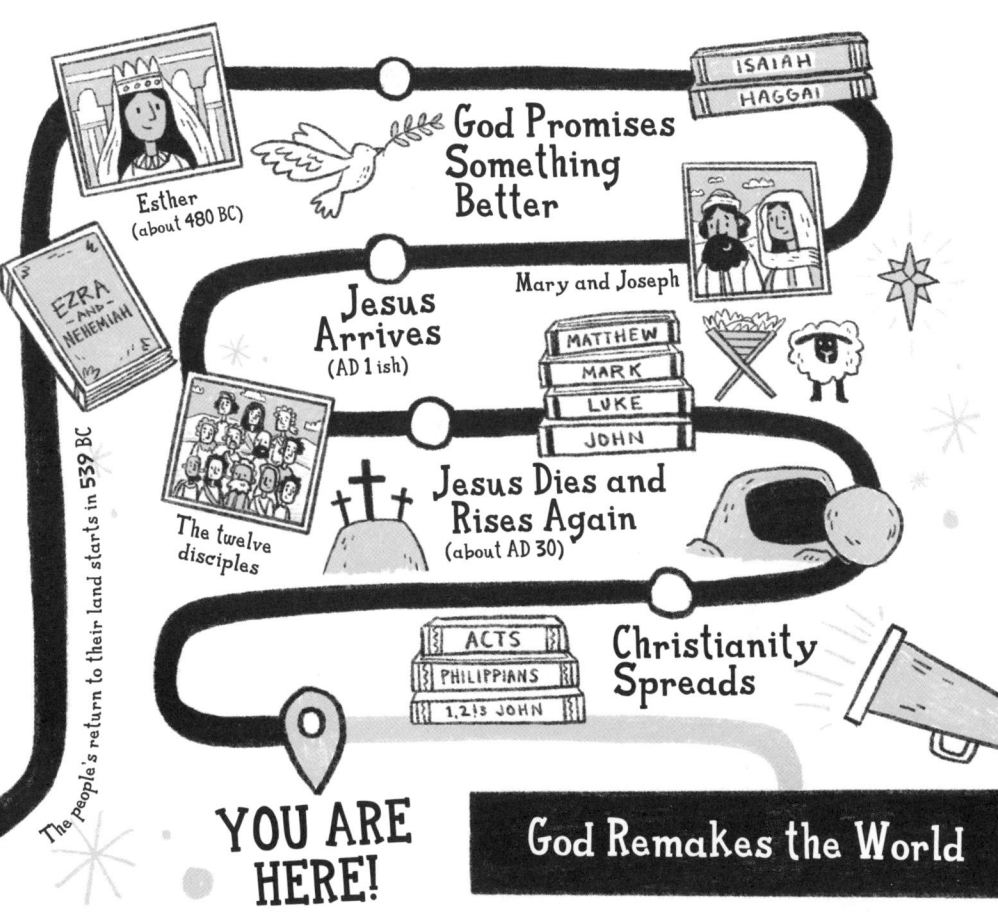

THE BIBLE IN A WEEK AND A HALF

Feeling brave? Try the whole Bible story in ten key passages—that's one per day for just a week and a half!

1. God creates the world
   Genesis 1 v 1-31
2. God chooses a people
   Genesis 12 v 1-7
3. God rescues his people
   Exodus 3 v 1-10
4. People keep messing up
   1 Kings 19 v 9-18
5. God punishes his people
   Jeremiah 25 v 1-11
6. God promises something better
   Isaiah 40 v 1-11
7. Jesus arrives
   Luke 1 v 26-38
8. Jesus dies and rises again
   Luke 24 v 1-8
9. Christianity spreads
   Acts 2 v 1-12
10. God remakes the world
    Revelation 21 v 1-4

MAPS

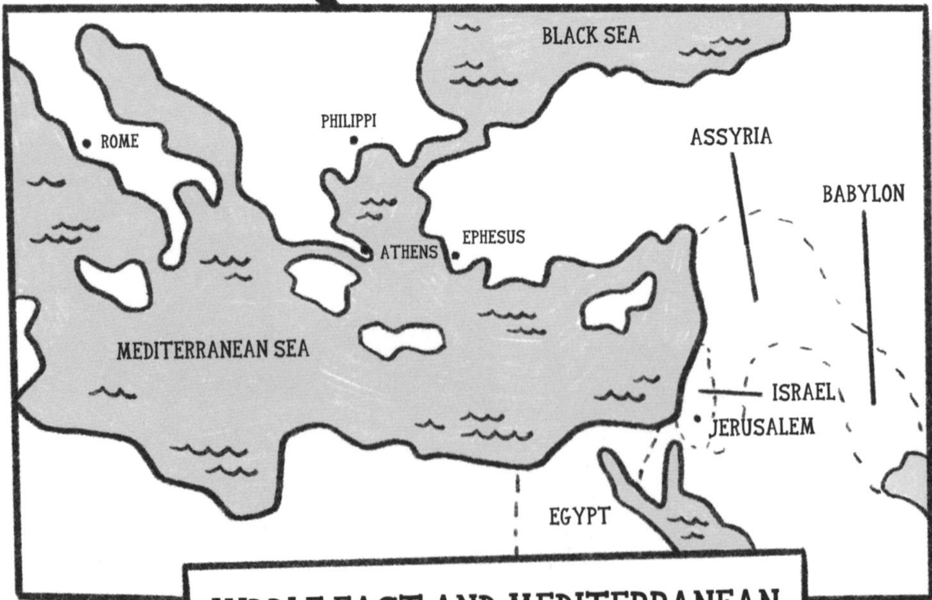

MIDDLE EAST AND MEDITERRANEAN

The Bible covers thousands of years, and in that time, places changed! Empires rose and fell. So these maps show some key places mentioned in the Bible, but you shouldn't assume they all existed at the same time.

The Old Testament focuses on things that happened in Israel and the Middle East, but the New Testament mentions places we think of as European, such as Rome and Athens. Paul and others travelled far and wide to spread the word about Jesus. Many New Testament letters are named after places—for example, Philippians was written to Christians who lived in Philippi.

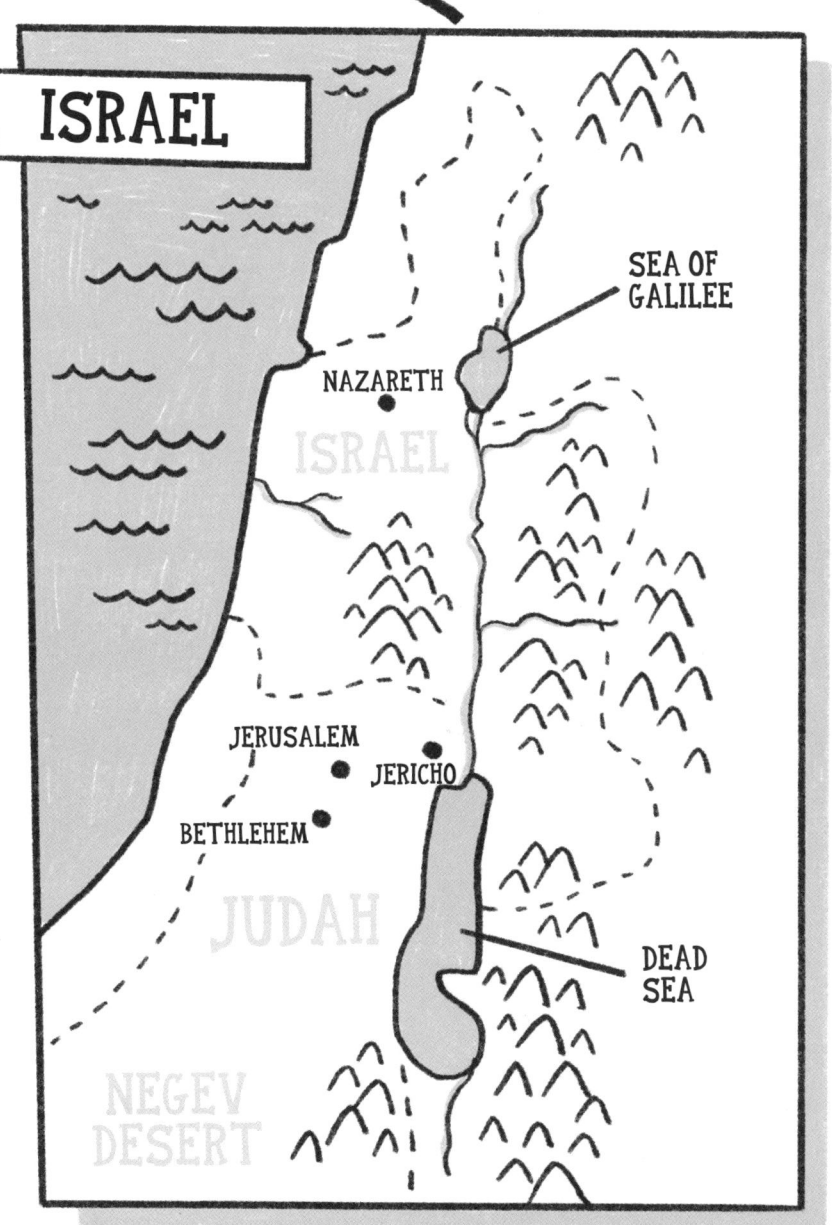

Israel was the name of God's people, but it ended up splitting into two kingdoms. One half was still called Israel, but the other half was called Judah. (Originally Judah was one of twelve tribes in Israel.) Later the land was split up differently by rulers like the Babylonians and Romans.

I HAVE QUESTIONS!

Q: Is the Bible really true? How do we know?

A: One way we know is because of other types of evidence. Archaeologists have found many objects from the past that fit with the Bible's account of history.

Another reason to believe the Bible is because you believe in Jesus. Many people have looked at the evidence that Jesus rose from the dead and decided it must have happened. If you believe that, it makes sense to believe the Bible.

Finally, many people are confident that the Bible is true simply because what it says just makes sense of how life is!

Q: Does the Bible contradict science?

A: Science is about how the physical world works, whereas the Bible is mostly about how we should live and what God is like. So they're not in conflict—they can work together to give us a deeper understanding of the world. It's very possible to love both science and the Bible!

Q: Why do different Christians believe different things if we're all learning from the same Bible?

A: The Bible is very clear about some things (e.g. Jesus died and rose), but doesn't have much to say on other things (e.g. art). So, Christians will disagree about art. They also sometimes disagree about things the Bible does talk about. Sometimes that's because the Bible isn't completely clear, and people interpret it differently. Sometimes it's because they aren't really listening to the Bible but putting forward their own opinions. The main thing is to agree that Jesus is our Lord and Saviour!

Q: Is it wrong to question the Bible and God?

A: No! Everyone has doubts sometimes. When we have questions, it's good to ask them. Find a Christian adult you trust, and ask! You'll probably find they have a good answer.

Q: What should we think about the bad things that happen in the Bible?

A: Not everything that happens in the Bible is good. Sometimes it tells you about a horrible thing that happened in history. It doesn't mean that's how God thinks life should be.

However, sometimes you may read about something that you don't like, but the Bible tells us that it is what God wanted (or still wants). That's hard! It's worth talking to God about—ask him to help you to trust that he is always good, and to understand what's going on in that passage.

Q: What is a Christian?

A: Romans 10 v 9 says, "If you declare with your mouth, 'Jesus is Lord,' and believe in your heart that God raised him from the dead, you will be saved." So, a Christian is someone who lives with Jesus as their Lord—that means they put him first and listen to him. And a Christian is someone who believes that Jesus died and rose again in order to save us.

Q: What is God really like?

A: This question will need more space! Turn the page to find out the answer…

WHAT IS GOD LIKE?

Many people believe in God or gods, but the Bible claims to tell us the truth about God. What the Bible says about God is different to what other religions say. Here are a few things we learn in the Bible about who God is and what he's like.

THE GOD OF CREATION

"In the beginning God created the heavens and the earth." —Genesis 1 v 1

When the Bible was written, most people believed in lots of different gods. But the Bible is clear that God is THE one and only true God. He's the most powerful being in the universe! The Bible starts with a description of how he made the whole world just by speaking.

THE GOD OF ISRAEL

"I am the Lord, the God of your father Abraham and the God of Isaac." —Genesis 28 v 13

Early on in the Bible, God chose Abraham's family (later called the Israelites) to be his own special people. God looked after the Israelites and was very loyal to them. It's not that he didn't love other people as well, but he had a special relationship with the Israelites!

THE GOD OF JUSTICE AND FORGIVENESS

God cares about how people live. He's perfectly loving, and so he hates it when people do unloving things! The amazing thing is that although God has extremely high standards for our behaviour, he's also very patient and forgiving when we get it wrong.

Here's how God once described himself to a man named Moses. Spot God's kindness and love, alongside his desire for justice:

> "The LORD, the LORD, the compassionate and gracious God, slow to anger, abounding in love and faithfulness, maintaining love to thousands, and forgiving wickedness, rebellion and sin. Yet he does not leave the guilty unpunished." —Exodus 34 v 6-7

THE GOD IN THREE PERSONS

God is one God. But the Bible reveals that he is also three "Persons"—God the Father, God the Son, and God the Holy Spirit. The three Persons seem to be separate: they talk to each other. Yet they're all the one God. It's a bit strange, but then, if God was easy to understand, he wouldn't be quite so amazing!

THE GOD WHO BECAME HUMAN

One of the three Persons is God the Son. That's Jesus! He is God, so he has always existed, but at the first Christmas he was born on earth as a baby. Jesus changed the way people relate to God. He took the punishment for every bad thing that has ever been done or ever will be done! If we trust in him, we become part of God's special, beloved people. We're not called Israelites anymore, though. We're called Christians.

BIBLE DICTIONARY

ANOINT   Anointing means pouring oil over someone's head! In Bible times, it was a way of saying, "This person is really special." When someone became king, he would be anointed instead of crowned.

AMEN   You've probably heard people saying this at the end of prayers. It literally means "truly". In other words, "I think that this is true!" When we say it in prayer, what we mean is "I agree with this" or "I really mean this".

COVENANT   This word pops up throughout the Bible. It means an agreement or promise that you can't get out of! God made a covenant with his people, promising to be loyal to them. Jesus made a new covenant—he changed the way we relate to God.

DISCIPLE   A follower or learner. A disciple is someone who really trusts their teacher and wants to hear everything he or she has to say. Christians today sometimes call themselves disciples of Jesus.

GOSPEL   This word means "good news". So, Christians talk about "the gospel of Jesus" or "the gospel message"—that means the good news about Jesus. There are also four books of the Bible called Gospels—they are the ones which tell us the good news about Jesus.

GRACE   This word basically means God's kindness to us. Another way of understanding it is to say that grace is when God gives us things that we don't deserve. For example, forgiveness is a gift of grace.

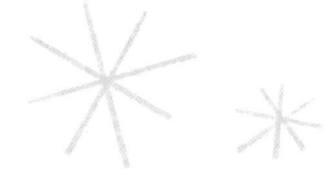

LORD You'll sometimes see this word printed in capital letters. Why? It signals that in the original Hebrew, the name of God has been used. This name is sometimes translated as Yahweh or Jehovah (because it sounds something like that in Hebrew), but it means "I am". It's in capitals so that we can tell the difference between this word and other words that mean "lord".

MESSIAH This word means "anointed one" or "chosen one". In the Old Testament, God promised to send the Messiah to sort out the world. In the New Testament, we find out that the Messiah is Jesus! Another word for Messiah is Christ.

REPENT This means to say sorry for what you have done wrong, and to turn away from it onto a new path.

SACRIFICE A sacrifice is when you give something up. In Old Testament times, people would kill animals or give up precious food, in order to show God that they loved him and wanted to follow him, or as a way of paying for what they had done wrong. We don't do this anymore because Jesus has sacrificed himself for us—which means that if we make Jesus the Lord of our lives, we already have a perfect relationship with God the Father, and we don't need to do anything else.

SIN A little word that means everything we do wrong. This can include any way in which we turn away from God and say no to what he tells us.

TEMPLE Temples are buildings whose purpose is to worship a god. In the Bible, God told his people to build the tabernacle, which was a huge tent-temple. Later, a proper building-temple was made. The temple was seen as God's house. Of course, God is everywhere, but the temple was a special place where people could come and talk to him. The Bible also talks about Jesus as a temple—and also everyone who follows him!

MORE HELP WITH BIBLE READING

Explores short Bible chunks, with puzzles!

Takes you through the life of Jesus

Fiction style retelling of the story of David

Gets you thinking about the Bible's overall storyline

Find all these and more at

thegoodbook.co.uk   thegoodbook.com